D1559256

MATTHEW ARNOLD

Selected Poems

BLOOMSBURY
* POETRY *
CLASSICS

This selection by Ian Hamilton
first published 1993
Copyright © 1993 by Bloomsbury Publishing Ltd

Bloomsbury Publishing Ltd, 2 Soho Square,
London W1V 5DE

A CIP catalogue record for this book is available from the
British Library

ISBN 0 7475 149 17

10 9 8 7 6 5 4 3 2 1

Typeset by Hewer Text Composition Services Limited,
Edinburgh
Printed in Great Britain by St Edmundsbury Press, Suffolk
Bound in Great Britain by Hunter and Foulis Limited
Edinburgh.

CONTENTS

6

LINES
WRITTEN IN KENSINGTON GARDENS

In this lone, open glade I lie,
Screen'd by deep boughs on either hand;
And at its end, to stay the eye,
Those black-crown'd, red-boled pine-trees stand!

Birds here make song, each bird has his,
Across the girdling city's hum.
How green under the boughs it is!
How thick the tremulous sheep-cries come!

Sometimes a child will cross the glade
To take his nurse his broken toy;
Sometimes a thrush flit overhead
Deep in her unknown day's employ.

Here at my feet what wonders pass,
What endless, active life is here!
What blowing daisies, fragrant grass!
An air-stirr'd forest, fresh and clear.

Scarce fresher is the mountain-sod
Where the tired angler lies, stretch'd out,
And, eased of basket and of rod,
Counts his day's spoil, the spotted trout.

In the huge world, which roars hard by,
Be others happy if they can!
But in my helpless cradle I
Was breathed on by the rural Pan.

I, on men's impious uproar hurl'd,
Think often, as I hear them rave,
That peace has left the upper world
And now keeps only in the grave.

Yet here is peace for ever new!
When I who watch them am away,
Still all things in this glade go through
The changes of their quiet day.

Then to their happy rest they pass!
The flowers upclose, the birds are fed,
The night comes down upon the grass,
The child sleeps warmly in his bed.

Calm soul of all things! make it mine
To feel, amid the city's jar,
That there abides a peace of thine,
Man did not make, and cannot mar.

The will to neither strive nor cry,
The power to feel with others give!
Calm, calm me more! nor let me die
Before I have begun to live.

From RESIGNATION
To Fausta

Once more we tread this self-same road,
Fausta, which ten years since we trod;
Alone we tread it, you and I,
Ghosts of that boisterous company.
Here, where the brook shines, near its head,
In its clear, shallow, turf-fringed bed;
Here, whence the eye first sees, far down,
Capp'd with faint smoke, the noisy town;
Here sit we, and again unroll,
Though slowly, the familiar whole.
The solemn wastes of heathy hill
Sleep in the July sunshine still;
The self-same shadows now, as then,
Play through this grassy upland glen;
The loose dark stones on the green way
Lie strewn, it seems, where then they lay;
On this mild bank above the stream,
(You crush them!) the blue gentians gleam.
Still this wild brook, the rushes cool,
The sailing foam, the shining pool!
These are not changed; and we, you say,
Are scarce more changed, in truth, than they.

The gipsies, whom we met below,
They, too, have long roam'd to and fro;
They ramble, leaving, where they pass,
Their fragments on the cumber'd grass.
And often to some kindly place
Chance guides the migratory race,
Where, though long wanderings intervene,
They recognise a former scene.
The dingy tents are pitch'd; the fires
Give to the wind their wavering spires;
In dark knots crouch round the wild flame
Their children, as when first they came;
They see their shackled beasts again
Move, browsing, up the gray-wall'd lane.
Signs are not wanting, which might raise
The ghost in them of former days –
Signs are not wanting, if they would;
Suggestions to disquietude.
For them, for all, time's busy touch,
While it mends little, troubles much.
Their joints grow stiffer – but the year
Runs his old round of dubious cheer;
Chilly they grow – yet winds in March,
Still, sharp as ever, freeze and parch;
They must live still – and yet, God knows,

Crowded and keen the country grows;
It seems as if, in their decay,
The law grew stronger every day.
So might they reason, so compare,
Fausta, times past with times that are.
But no! – they rubb'd through yesterday
In their hereditary way,
And they will rub through, if they can,
To-morrow on the self-same plan,
Till death arrive to supersede,
For them, vicissitude and need.

The poet, to whose mighty heart
Heaven doth a quicker pulse impart,
Subdues that energy to scan
Not his own course, but that of man.
Though he move mountains, though his day
Be pass'd on the proud heights of sway,
Though he hath loosed a thousand chains,
Though he hath borne immortal pains,
Action and suffering though he know –
He hath not lived, if he lives so.
He sees, in some great-historied land,
A ruler of the people stand,
Sees his strong thought in fiery flood
Roll through the heaving multitude;

Exults – yet for no moment's space
Envies the all-regarded place.
Beautiful eyes meet his – and he
Bears to admire uncravingly;
They pass – he, mingled with the crowd,
Is in their far-off triumphs proud.
From some high station he looks down,
At sunset, on a populous town;
Surveys each happy group, which fleets,
Toil ended, through the shining streets,
Each with some errand of its own –
And does not say: *I am alone.*

He sees the gentle stir of birth
When morning purifies the earth;
He leans upon a gate and sees
The pastures, and the quiet trees.
Low, woody hill, with gracious bound,
Folds the still valley almost round;
The cuckoo, loud on some high lawn,
Is answer'd from the depth of dawn;
In the hedge straggling to the stream,
Pale, dew-drench'd, half-shut roses gleam;
But, where the farther side slopes down,
He sees the drowsy new-waked clown

In his white quaint-embroider'd frock
Make, whistling, tow'rd his mist-wreathed flock –
Slowly, behind his heavy tread,
The wet, flower'd grass heaves up its head.
Lean'd on his gate, he gazes – tears
Are in his eyes, and in his ears
The murmur of a thousand years.
Before him he sees life unroll,
A placid and continuous whole –
That general life, which does not cease,
Whose secret is not joy, but peace;
That life, whose dumb wish is not miss'd
If birth proceeds, if things subsist;
The life of plants, and stones, and rain,
The life he craves – if not in vain
Fate gave, what chance shall not control,
His sad lucidity of soul.

. . .

From STANZAS IN MEMORY OF THE
AUTHOR OF OBERMANN

Some secrets may the poet tell,
For the world loves new ways;
To tell too deep ones is not well –
It knows not what he says.

Yet of the spirits who have reign'd
In this our troubled day,
I know but two, who have attain'd,
Save thee, to see their way.

By England's lakes, in grey old age,
His quiet home one keeps;
And one, the strong much-toiling sage,
In German Weimar sleeps.

But Wordsworth's eyes avert their ken
From half of human fate;
And Goethe's course few sons of men
May think to emulate.

For he pursued a lonely road,
His eyes on Nature's plan;
Neither made man too much a God,
Nor God too much a man.

Strong was he, with a spirit free
From mists, and sane, and clear;
Clearer, how much! than ours – yet we
Have a worse course to steer.

For though his manhood bore the blast
Of a tremendous time,
Yet in a tranquil world was pass'd
His tenderer youthful prime.

But we, brought forth and rear'd in hours
Of change, alarm, surprise –
What shelter to grow ripe is ours?
What leisure to grow wise?

Like children bathing on the shore,
Buried a wave beneath,
The second wave succeeds, before
We have had time to breathe.

Too fast we live, too much are tried,
Too harass'd, to attain
Wordsworth's sweet calm, or Goethe's wide
And luminous view to gain.

And then we turn, thou sadder sage,
To thee! we feel thy spell!
– The hopeless tangle of our age,
Thou too hast scann'd it well!

Immoveable thou sittest, still
As death, composed to bear!
Thy head is clear, thy feeling chill,
And icy thy despair.

Yes, as the son of Thetis said,
I hear thee saying now:
Greater by far than thou are dead;
Strive not! die also thou!

Ah! two desires toss about
The poet's feverish blood.
One drives him to the world without,
And one to solitude.

The glow, he cries, *the thrill of life,*
Where, where do these abound? –
Not in the world, not in the strife
Of men, shall they be found.

He who hath watch'd, not shared, the strife,
Knows how the day hath gone.
He only lives with the world's life,
Who hath renounced his own.

. . .

SWITZERLAND

1. MEETING

Again I see my bliss at hand,
The town, the lake are here;
My Marguerite smiles upon the strand,
Unalter'd with the year.

I know that graceful figure fair,
That cheek of languid hue;
I know that soft, enkerchief'd hair,
And those sweet eyes of blue.

Again I spring to make my choice;
Again in tones of ire
I hear a God's tremendous voice:
'Be counsell'd, and retire.'

Ye guiding Powers who join and part,
What would ye have with me?
Ah, warn some more ambitious heart,
And let the peaceful be!

2. PARTING

Ye storm-winds of Autumn!
Who rush by, who shake
The window, and ruffle
The gleam-lighted lake;
Who cross to the hill-side
Thin-sprinkled with farms,
Where the high woods strip sadly
Their yellowing arms –
Ye are bound for the mountains!
Ah! with you let me go
Where your cold, distant barrier,
The vast range of snow,
Through the loose clouds lifts dimly
Its white peaks in the air –
How deep is their stillness!
Ah, would I were there!

But on the stairs what voice is this I hear,
Buoyant as morning, and as morning clear?
Say, has some wet bird-haunted English lawn
Lent it the music of its trees at dawn?
Or was it from some sun-fleck'd mountain-brook
That the sweet voice its upland clearness took?
      Ah! it comes nearer –
      Sweet notes, this way!

    Hark! fast by the window
    The rushing winds go,
    To the ice-cumber'd gorges,
    The vast seas of snow!
    There the torrents drive upward
    Their rock-strangled hum;
    There the avalanche thunders
    The hoarse torrent dumb.
    – I come, O ye mountains!
    Ye torrents, I come!

But who is this, by the half-open'd door,
Whose figure casts a shadow on the floor?
The sweet blue eyes – the soft, ash-colour'd hair –
The cheeks that still their gentle paleness wear –
The lovely lips, with their arch smile that tells
The unconquer'd joy in which her spirit dwells –
      Ah! they bend nearer –
      Sweet lips, this way!

    Hark! the wind rushes past us!
    Ah! with that let me go
    To the clear, waning hill-side,
    Unspotted by snow,
    There to watch, o'er the sunk vale,
    The frore mountain-wall,
    Where the niched snow-bed sprays down
    Its powdery fall.
    There its dusky blue clusters
    The aconite spreads;
    There the pines slope, the cloud-strips
    Hung soft in their heads.
    No life but, at moments,
    The mountain-bee's hum.
    – I come, O ye mountains!
    Ye pine-woods, I come!

Forgive me! forgive me!
  Ah, Marguerite, fain
Would these arms reach to clasp thee!
  But see! 'tis in vain.

In the void air, towards thee,
  My stretch'd arms are cast;
But a sea rolls between us –
  Our different past!

To the lips, ah! of others
  Those lips have been prest,
And others, ere I was,
  Were strain'd to that breast;

Far, far from each other
  Our spirits have grown;
And what heart knows another?
  Ah! who knows his own?

Blow, ye winds! lift me with you!
  I come to the wild.
Fold closely, O Nature!
  Thine arms round thy child.

To thee only God granted
   A heart ever new –
To all always open,
   To all always true.

Ah! calm me, restore me;
   And dry up my tears
On thy high mountain-platforms,
   Where morn first appears;

Where the white mists, for ever,
   Are spread and upfurl'd –
In the stir of the forces
   Whence issued the world.

3. A FAREWELL

My horse's feet beside the lake,
Where sweet the unbroken moonbeams lay,
Sent echoes through the night to wake
Each glistening strand, each heath-fringed bay.

The poplar avenue was pass'd,
And the roof'd bridge that spans the stream;
Up the steep street I hurried fast,
Led by thy taper's starlike beam.

I came! I saw thee rise! – the blood
Pour'd flushing to thy languid cheek.
Lock'd in each other's arms we stood,
In tears, with hearts too full to speak.

Days flew; – ah, soon I could discern
A trouble in thine alter'd air!
Thy hand lay languidly in mine,
Thy cheek was grave, thy speech grew rare.

I blame thee not! – this heart, I know,
To be long loved was never framed;
For something in its depths doth glow
Too strange, too restless, too untamed.

And women – things that live and move
Mined by the fever of the soul –
They seek to find in those they love
Stern strength, and promise of control.

They ask not kindness, gentle ways –
These they themselves have tried and known;
They ask a soul which never sways
With the blind gusts that shake their own.

I too have felt the load I bore
In a too strong emotion's sway;
I too have wish'd, no woman more,
This starting, feverish heart away.

I too have long'd for trenchant force,
And will like a dividing spear;
Have praised the keen, unscrupulous course,
Which knows no doubt, which feels no fear.

But in the world I learnt, what there
Thou too wilt surely one day prove,
That will, that energy, though rare,
Are yet far, far less rare than love.

Go, then! – till time and fate impress
This truth on thee, be mine no more!
They will! – for thou, I feel, not less
Than I, wast destined to this lore.

We school our manners, act our parts –
But He, who sees us through and through,
Knows that the bent of both our hearts
Was to be gentle, tranquil, true.

And though we wear out life, alas!
Distracted as a homeless wind,
In beating where we must not pass,
In seeking what we shall not find;

Yet we shall one day gain, life past,
Clear prospect o'er our being's whole;
Shall see ourselves, and learn at last
Our true affinities of soul.

We shall not then deny a course
To every thought the mass ignore;
We shall not then call hardness force,
Nor lightness wisdom any more.

Then, in the eternal Father's smile,
Our soothed, encouraged souls will dare
To seem as free from pride and guile,
As good, as generous, as they are.

Then we shall know our friends! – though much
Will have been lost – the help in strife,
The thousand sweet, still joys of such
As hand in hand face earthly life –

Though these be lost, there will be yet
A sympathy august and pure;
Ennobled by a vast regret,
And by contrition seal'd thrice sure.

And we, whose ways were unlike here,
May then more neighbouring courses ply;
May to each other be brought near,
And greet across infinity.

How sweet, unreach'd by earthly jars,
My sister! to maintain with thee
The hush among the shining stars,
The calm upon the moonlit sea!

How sweet to feel, on the boon air,
All our unquiet pulses cease!
To feel that nothing can impair
The gentleness, the thirst for peace –

The gentleness too rudely hurl'd
On this wild earth of hate and fear;
The thirst for peace a raving world
Would never let us satiate here.

4. ISOLATION – TO MARGUERITE

We were apart; yet, day by day,
I bade my heart more constant be.
I bade it keep the world away,
And grow a home for only thee;
Nor fear'd but thy love likewise grew,
Like mine, each day, more tried, more true.

The fault was grave! I might have known,
What far too soon, alas! I learn'd –
The heart can bind itself alone,
And faith may oft be unreturn'd.
Self-sway'd our feelings ebb and swell –
Thou lov'st no more; – Farewell! Farewell!

Farewell! – and thou, thou lonely heart,
Which never yet without remorse
Even for a moment didst depart
From thy remote and spheréd course
To haunt the place where passions reign –
Back to thy solitude again!

Back! with the conscious thrill of shame
Which Luna felt, that summer-night,
Flash through her pure immortal frame,
When she forsook the starry height
To hang over Endymion's sleep
Upon the pine-grown Latmian steep.

Yet she, chaste queen, had never proved
How vain a thing is mortal love,
Wandering in Heaven, far removed.
But thou hast long had place to prove
This truth – to prove, and make thine own:
'Thou hast been, shalt be, art, alone.'

Or, if not quite alone, yet they
Which touch thee are unmating things –
Ocean and clouds and night and day;
Lorn autumns and triumphant springs;
And life, and others' joy and pain,
And love, if love, of happier men.

Of happier men – for they, at least,
Have *dream'd* two human hearts might blend
In one, and were through faith released
From isolation without end
Prolong'd; nor knew, although not less
Alone than thou, their loneliness.

Yes! in the sea of life enisled,
With echoing straits between us thrown,
Dotting the shoreless watery wild,
We mortal millions live *alone*.
The islands feel the enclasping flow,
And then their endless bounds they know.

But when the moon their hollows lights,
And they are swept by balms of spring,
And in their glens, on starry nights,
The nightingales divinely sing;
And lovely notes, from shore to shore,
Across the sounds and channels pour –

Oh! then a longing like despair
Is to their farthest caverns sent;
For surely once, they feel, we were
Parts of a single continent!
Now round us spreads the watery plain –
Oh might our marges meet again!

Who order'd, that their longing's fire
Should be, as soon as kindled, cool'd?
Who renders vain their deep desire? –
A God, a God their severance ruled!
And bade betwixt their shores to be
The unplumb'd, salt, estranging sea.

6. ABSENCE

In this fair stranger's eyes of grey
Thine eyes, my love! I see.
I shiver; for the passing day
Had borne me far from thee.

This is the curse of life! that not
A nobler, calmer train
Of wiser thoughts and feelings blot
Our passions from our brain;

But each day brings its petty dust
Our soon-choked souls to fill,
And we forget because we must
And not because we will.

I struggle towards the light; and ye,
Once-long'd-for storms of love!
If with the light ye cannot be,
I bear that ye remove.

I struggle towards the light – but oh,
While yet the night is chill,
Upon time's barren, stormy flow,
Stay with me, Marguerite, still!

7. THE TERRACE AT BERNE
(Composed ten years after the preceding.)

Ten years! – and to my waking eye
Once more the roofs of Berne appear;
The rocky banks, the terrace high,
The stream! – and do I linger here?

The clouds are on the Oberland,
The Jungfrau snows look faint and far;
But bright are those green fields at hand,
And through those fields comes down the Aar,

And from the blue twin-lakes it comes,
Flows by the town, the churchyard fair;
And 'neath the garden-walk it hums,
The house! – and is my Marguerite there?

Ah, shall I see thee, while a flush
Of startled pleasure floods thy brow,
Quick through the oleanders brush,
And clap thy hands, and cry: *'Tis thou!*

Or hast thou long since wander'd back,
Daughter of France! to France, thy home;
And flitted down the flowery track
Where feet like thine too lightly come?

Doth riotous laughter now replace
Thy smile; and rouge, with stony glare,
Thy cheek's soft hue; and fluttering lace
The kerchief that enwound thy hair?

Or is it over? – art thou dead? –
Dead! – and no warning shiver ran
Across my heart, to say thy thread
Of life was cut, and closed thy span!

Could from earth's ways that figure slight
Be lost, and I not feel 'twas so?
Of that fresh voice the gay delight
Fail from earth's air, and I not know?

Or shall I find thee still, but changed,
But not the Marguerite of thy prime?
With all thy being re-arranged,
Pass'd through the crucible of time;

With spirit vanish'd, beauty waned,
And hardly yet a glance, a tone,
A gesture – anything – retain'd
Of all that was my Marguerite's own?

I will not know! For wherefore try,
To things by mortal course that live,
A shadowy durability,
For which they were not meant, to give?

Like driftwood spars, which meet and pass
Upon the boundless ocean-plain,
So on the sea of life, alas!
Man meets man – meets, and quits again.

I knew it when my life was young;
I feel it still, now youth is o'er.
– The mists are on the mountain hung,
And Marguerite I shall see no more.

FADED LEAVES

1. THE RIVER

Still glides the stream, slow drops the boat
Under the rustling poplars' shade;
Silent the swans beside us float –
None speaks, none heeds; ah, turn thy head!

Let those arch eyes now softly shine,
That mocking mouth grow sweetly bland;
Ah, let them rest, those eyes, on mine!
On mine let rest that lovely hand!

My pent-up tears oppress my brain,
My heart is swoln with love unsaid.
Ah, let me weep, and tell my pain,
And on thy shoulder rest my head!

Before I die – before the soul,
Which now is mine, must re-attain
Immunity from my control,
And wander round the world again;

Before this teased o'erlabour'd heart
For ever leaves its vain employ,
Dead to its deep habitual smart,
And dead to hopes of future joy.

5. LONGING

Come to me in my dreams, and then
By day I shall be well again!
For then the night will more than pay
The hopeless longing of the day.

Come, as thou cam'st a thousand times,
A messenger from radiant climes,
And smile on thy new world, and be
As kind to others as to me!

Or, as thou never cam'st in sooth,
Come now, and let me dream it truth;
And part my hair, and kiss my brow,
And say: *My love! why sufferest thou?*

Come to me in my dreams, and then
By day I shall be well again!
For then the night will more than pay
The hopeless longing of the day.

From EMPEDOCLES ON ETNA

Empedocles

And lie thou there,
My laurel bough!
Scornful Apollo's ensign, lie thou there!
Though thou hast been my shade in the world's
    heat –
Though I have loved thee, lived in honouring thee –
Yet lie thou there,
My laurel bough!

I am weary of thee.
I am weary of the solitude.
Where he who bears thee must abide –
Of the rocks of Parnassus,
Of the gorge of Delphi,
Of the moonlit peaks, and the caves.
Thou guardest them, Apollo!
Over the grave of the slain Pytho,
Though young, intolerably severe!
Thou keepest aloof the profane,
But the solitude oppresses thy votary!
The jars of men reach him not in thy valley –
But can life reach him?

Thou fencest him from the multitude –
Who will fence him from himself?
He hears nothing but the cry of the torrents,
And the beating of his own heart.
The air is thin, the veins swell,
The temples tighten and throb there –
Air! air!

Take thy bough, set me free from my solitude;
I have been enough alone!

Where shall thy votary fly then? back to men? –
But they will gladly welcome him once more,
And help him to unbend his too tense thought,
And rid him of the presence of himself,
And keep their friendly chatter at his ear,
And haunt him, till the absence from himself,
That other torment, grow unbearable;
And he will fly to solitude again,
And he will find its air too keen for him,
And so change back; and many thousand times
Be miserably bandied to and fro
Like a sea-wave, betwixt the world and thee,
Thou young, implacable God! and only death
Can cut his oscillations short, and so
Bring him to poise. There is no other way.

And yet what days were those, Parmenides!
When we were young, when we could number friends
In all the Italian cities like ourselves,
When with elated hearts we join'd your train,
Ye Sun-born Virgins! on the road of truth.
Then we could still enjoy, then neither thought
Nor outward things were closed and dead to us;
But we received the shock of mighty thoughts
On simple minds with a pure natural joy;
And if the sacred load oppress'd our brain,
We had the power to feel the pressure eased,
The brow unbound, the thoughts flow free again,
In the delightful commerce of the world.
We had not lost our balance then, nor grown
Thought's slaves, and dead to every natural joy.
The smallest thing could give us pleasure then –
The sports of the country-people,
A flute-note from the woods,
Sunset over the sea;
Seed-time and harvest,
The reapers in the corn,
The vinedresser in his vineyard,
The village-girl at her wheel.

Fulness of life and power of feeling, ye
Are for the happy, for the souls at ease,
Who dwell on a firm basis of content!
But he, who has outlived his prosperous days –
But he, whose youth fell on a different world
From that on which his exiled age is thrown –
Whose mind was fed on other food, was train'd
By other rules than are in vogue to-day –
Whose habit of thought is fix'd, who will not change,
But, in a world he loves not, must subsist
In ceaseless opposition, be the guard
Of his own breast, fetter'd to what he guards,
That the world win no mastery over him –
Who has no friend, no fellow left, not one;
Who has no minute's breathing space allow'd
To nurse his dwindling faculty of joy –
Joy and the outward world must die to him,
As they are dead to me.

A long pause, during which EMPEDOCLES *remains
    motionless, plunged in thought. The night deepens. He moves
    forward and gazes round him, and proceeds:* –

And you, ye stars,
Who slowly begin to marshal,
As of old, in the fields of heaven,
Your distant, melancholy lines!
Have you, too, survived yourselves?
Are you, too, what I fear to become?
You, too, once lived;
You, too, moved joyfully
Among august companions,
In an older world, peopled by Gods,
In a mightier order,
The radiant, rejoicing, intelligent Sons of Heaven.
But now, ye kindle
Your lonely, cold-shining lights,
Unwilling lingerers
In the heavenly wilderness,
For a younger, ignoble world;
And renew, by necessity,
Night after night your courses,
In echoing, unnear'd silence,
Above a race you know not –
Uncaring and undelighted,
Without friend and without home;
Weary like us, though not
Weary with our weariness.

No, no, ye stars! there is no death with you,
No languor, no decay! languor and death,
They are with me, not you! ye are alive –
Ye, and the pure dark ether where ye ride
Brilliant above me! And thou, fiery world,
That sapp'st the vitals of this terrible mount
Upon whose charr'd and quaking crust I stand –
Thou, too, brimmest with life! – the sea of cloud,
That heaves its white and billowy vapours up
To moat this isle of ashes from the world,
Lives; and that other fainter sea, far down,
O'er whose lit floor a road of moonbeams leads
To Etna's Liparëan sister-fires
And the long dusky line of Italy –
That mild and luminous floor of waters lives,
With held-in joy swelling its heart; I only,
Whose spring of hope is dried, whose spirit has fail'd,
I, who have not, like these, in solitude
Maintain'd courage and force, and in myself
Nursed an immortal vigour – I alone
Am dead to life and joy, therefore I read
In all things my own deadness.

A long silence. He continues: –

Oh, that I could glow like this mountain!
Oh, that my heart bounded with the swell of the sea!
Oh, that my soul were full of light as the stars!
Oh, that it brooded over the world like the air!

But no, this heart will glow no more; thou art
A living man no more, Empedocles!
Nothing but a devouring flame of thought –
But a naked, eternally restless mind!

After a pause: –

To the elements it came from
Everything will return –
Our bodies to earth,
Our blood to water,
Heat to fire,
Breath to air.
They were well born, they will be well entomb'd –
But mind? . . .
And we might gladly share the fruitful stir
Down in our mother earth's miraculous womb;
Well would it be
With what roll'd of us in the stormy main;
We might have joy, blent with the all-bathing air,
Or with the nimble, radiant life of fire.

But mind, but thought –
If these have been the master part of us –
Where will *they* find their parent element?
What will receive *them*, who will call *them* home?
But we shall still be in them, and they in us,
And we shall be the strangers of the world,
And they will be our lords, as they are now;
And keep us prisoners of our consciousness,
And never let us clasp and feel the All
But through their forms, and modes, and stifling veils.
And we shall be unsatisfied as now;
And we shall feel the agony of thirst,
The ineffable longing for the life of life
Baffled for ever; and still thought and mind
Will hurry us with them on their homeless march,
Over the unallied unopening earth,
Over the unrecognizing sea; while air
Will blow us fiercely back to sea and earth,
And fire repel us from its living waves.
And then we shall unwillingly return
Back to this meadow of calamity,
This uncongenial place, this human life;
And in our individual human state
Go through the sad probation all again,
To see if we will poise our life at last,

To see if we will now at last be true
To our own only true, deep-buried selves,
Being one with which we are one with the whole
    world;
Or whether we will once more fall away
Into some bondage of the flesh or mind,
Some slough of sense, or some fantastic maze
Forged by the imperious lonely thinking-power.
And each succeeding age in which we are born
Will have more peril for us than the last;
Will goad our senses with a sharper spur,
Will fret our minds to an intenser play,
Will make ourselves harder to be discern'd.
And we shall struggle awhile, gasp and rebel –
And we shall fly for refuge to past times,
Their soul of unworn youth, their breath of greatness;
And the reality will pluck us back,
Knead us in its hot hand, and change our nature
And we shall feel our powers of effort flag,
And rally them for one last fight – and fail;
And we shall sink in the impossible strife,
And be astray for ever.

. . .

From TRISTRAM AND ISEULT
PART III

. . .

And is she happy? Does she see unmoved
The days in which she might have lived and loved
Slip without bringing bliss slowly away,
One after one, to-morrow like to-day?
Joy has not found her yet, nor ever will –
Is it this thought which makes her mien so still,
Her features so fatigued, her eyes, though sweet,
So sunk, so rarely lifted save to meet
Her children's? She moves slow; her voice alone
Hath yet an infantine and silver tone,
But even that comes languidly; in truth,
She seems one dying in a mask of youth.
And now she will go home, and softly lay
Her laughing children in their beds, and play
Awhile with them before they sleep; and then
She'll light her silver lamp, which fishermen
Dragging their nets through the rough waves, afar,
Along this iron coast, know like a star,
And take her broidery-frame, and there she'll sit
Hour after hour, her gold curls sweeping it;
Lifting her soft-bent head only to mind
Her children, or to listen to the wind.

And when the clock peals midnight, she will move
Her work away, and let her fingers rove
Across the shaggy brows of Tristram's hound
Who lies, guarding her feet, along the ground;
Or else she will fall musing, her blue eyes
Fixt, her slight hands clasp'd on her lap; then rise,
And at her prie-dieu kneel, until she have told
Her rosary-beads of ebony tipp'd with gold,
Then to her soft sleep – and to-morrow'll be
To-day's exact repeated effigy.

Yes, it is lonely for her in her hall.
The children, and the grey-hair'd seneschal,
Her women, and Sir Tristram's aged hound,
Are there the sole companions to be found.
But these she loves; and noisier life than this
She would find ill to bear, weak as she is.

She has her children, too, and night and day
Is with them; and the wide heaths where they play,
The hollies, and the cliff, and the sea-shore,
The sand, the sea-birds, and the distant sails,
These are to her dear as to them; the tales
With which this day the children she beguiled
She gleaned from Breton grandames, when a child,
In every hut along this sea-coast wild.
She herself loves them still, and, when they are told,
Can forget all to hear them, as of old.

Dear saints, it is not sorrow, as I hear,
Not suffering, which shuts up eye and ear
To all that has delighted them before,
And lets us be what we were once no more.
No, we may suffer deeply, yet retain
Power to be moved and soothed, for all our pain,
By what of old pleased us, and will again.

No, 'tis the gradual furnace of the world,
In whose hot air our spirits are upcurl'd
Until they crumble, or else grow like steel –
Which kills in us the bloom, the youth, the spring –
Which leaves the fierce necessity to feel,
But takes away the power – this can avail,
By drying up our joy in everything,
To make our former pleasures all seem stale.
This, or some tyrannous single thought, some fit
Of passion, which subdues our souls to it,
Till for its sake alone we live and move –
Call it ambition, or remorse, or love –
This too can change us wholly, and make seem
All which we did before, shadow and dream.

. . .

DOVER BEACH

The sea is calm to-night.
The tide is full, the moon lies fair
Upon the straits; – on the French coast the light
Gleams and is gone; the cliffs of England stand,
Glimmering and vast, out in the tranquil bay.
Come to the window, sweet is the night-air!
Only, from the long line of spray
Where the sea meets the moon-blanch'd land,
Listen! you hear the grating roar
Of pebbles which the waves draw back, and fling,
At their return, up the high strand,
Begin, and cease, and then again begin,
With tremulous cadence slow, and bring
The eternal note of sadness in.

Sophocles long ago
Heard it on the Aegaean, and it brought
Into his mind the turbid ebb and flow
Of human misery; we
Find also in the sound a thought,
Hearing it by this distant northern sea.

The Sea of Faith
Was once, too, at the full, and round earth's shore
Lay like the folds of a bright girdle furl'd.
But now I only hear
Its melancholy, long, withdrawing roar,
Retreating, to the breath
Of the night-wind, down the vast edges drear
And naked shingles of the world.

Ah, love, let us be true
To one another! for the world, which seems
To lie before us like a land of dreams,
So various, so beautiful, so new,
Hath really neither joy, nor love, nor light,
Nor certitude, nor peace, nor help for pain;
And we are here as on a darkling plain
Swept with confused alarms of struggle and flight,
Where ignorant armies clash by night.

A SUMMER NIGHT

In the deserted, moon-blanch'd street,
How lonely rings the echo of my feet!
Those windows, which I gaze at, frown,
Silent and white, unopening down,
Repellent as the world; – but see,
A break between the housetops shows
The moon! and, lost behind her, fading dim
Into the dewy dark obscurity
Down at the far horizon's rim,
Doth a whole tract of heaven disclose!

And to my mind the thought
Is on a sudden brought
Of a past night, and a far different scene.
Headlands stood out into the moonlit deep
As clearly as at noon;
The spring-tide's brimming flow
Heaved dazzlingly between;
Houses, with long white sweep,
Girdled the glistening bay;
Behind, through the soft air,
The blue haze-cradled mountains spread away,
That night was far more fair –
But the same restless pacings to and fro,
And the same vainly throbbing heart was there,
And the same bright, calm moon.

And the calm moonlight seems to say:
Hast thou then still the old unquiet breast,
Which neither deadens into rest,
Nor ever feels the fiery glow
That whirls the spirit from itself away,
But fluctuates to and fro,
Never by passion quite possess'd
And never quite benumb'd by the world's sway? –
And I, I know not if to pray
Still to be what I am, or yield and be
Like all the other men I see.

For most men in a brazen prison live,
Where, in the sun's hot eye,
With heads bent o'er their toil, they languidly
Their lives to some unmeaning taskwork give,
Dreaming of nought beyond their prison-wall.
And as, year after year,
Fresh products of their barren labour fall
From their tired hands, and rest
Never yet comes more near,
Gloom settles slowly down over their breast;
And while they try to stem
The waves of mournful thought by which they are
    prest,
Death in their prison reaches them,
Unfreed, having seen nothing, still unblest.

And the rest, a few,
Escape their prison and depart
On the wide ocean of life anew.
There the freed prisoner, where'er his heart
Listeth, will sail;
Nor doth he know how there prevail,
Despotic on that sea,
Trade-winds which cross it from eternity.
Awhile he holds some false way, undebarr'd
By thwarting signs, and braves
The freshening wind and blackening waves.
And then the tempest strikes him; and between
The lightning-bursts is seen
Only a driving wreck,
And the pale master on his spar-strewn deck
With anguish'd face and flying hair
Grasping the rudder hard,
Still bent to make some port he knows not where,
Still standing for some false, impossible shore.
And sterner comes the roar
Of sea and wind, and through the deepening gloom
Fainter and fainter wreck and helmsman loom,
And he too disappears, and comes no more.

Is there no life, but these alone?
Madman or slave, must man be one?

Plainness and clearness without shadow of stain!
Clearness divine!
Ye heavens, whose pure dark regions have no sign
Of languor, though so calm, and, though so great,
Are yet untroubled and unpassionate;
Who, though so noble, share in the world's toil,
And, though so task'd, keep free from dust and soil!
I will not say that your mild deeps retain
A tinge, it may be, of their silent pain
Who have long'd deeply once, and long'd in vain –
But I will rather say that you remain
A world above man's head, to let him see
How boundless might his soul's horizons be,
How vast, yet of what clear transparency!
How it were good to abide there, and breathe free;
How fair a lot to fill
Is left to each man still!

THE BURIED LIFE

Light flows our war of mocking words, and yet,
Behold, with tears mine eyes are wet!
I feel a nameless sadness o'er me roll.
Yes, yes, we know that we can jest,
We know, we know that we can smile!
But there's a something in this breast,
To which thy light words bring no rest,
And thy gay smiles no anodyne.
Give me thy hand, and hush awhile,
And turn those limpid eyes on mine,
And let me read there, love! thy inmost soul.

Alas! is even love too weak
To unlock the heart, and let it speak?
Are even lovers powerless to reveal
To one another what indeed they feel?
I knew the mass of men conceal'd
Their thoughts, for fear that if reveal'd
They would by other men be met
With blank indifference, or with blame reproved;
I knew they lived and moved
Trick'd in disguises, alien to the rest
Of men, and alien to themselves – and yet
The same heart beats in every human breast!

But we, my love! – doth a like spell benumb
Our hearts, our voices? – must we too be dumb?

Ah! well for us, if even we,
Even for a moment, can get free
Our heart, and have our lips unchain'd;
For that which seals them hath been deep-ordain'd!

Fate, which foresaw
How frivolous a baby man would be –
By what distractions he would be possess'd,
How he would pour himself in every strife,
And well-nigh change his own identity --
That it might keep from his capricious play
His genuine self, and force him to obey
Even in his own despite his being's law,
Bade through the deep recesses of our breast
The unregarded river of our life
Pursue with indiscernible flow its way;
And that we should not see
The buried stream, and seem to be
Eddying at large in blind uncertainty,
Though driving on with it eternally.

But often, in the world's most crowded streets,
But often, in the din of strife,
There rises an unspeakable desire
After the knowledge of our buried life;

A thirst to spend our fire and restless force
In tracking out our true, original course;
A longing to inquire
Into the mystery of this heart which beats
So wild, so deep in us – to know
Whence our lives come and where they go.
And many a man in his own breast then delves,
But deep enough, alas! none ever mines.
And we have been on many thousand lines,
And we have shown, on each, spirit and power;
But hardly have we, for one little hour,
Been on our own line, have we been ourselves –
Hardly had skill to utter one of all
The nameless feelings that course through our breast,
But they course on for ever unexpress'd.
And long we try in vain to speak and act
Our hidden self, and what we say and do
Is eloquent, is well – but 'tis not true!
And then we will no more be rack'd
With inward striving, and demand
Of all the thousand nothings of the hour
Their stupefying power;
Ah yes, and they benumb us at our call!
Yet still, from time to time, vague and forlorn,
From the soul's subterranean depth upborne
As from an infinitely distant land,
Come airs, and floating echoes, and convey

A melancholy into all our day.
Only – but this is rare –
When a belovéd hand is laid in ours,
When, jaded with the rush and glare
Of the interminable hours,
Our eyes can in another's eyes read clear,
When our world-deafen'd ear
Is by the tones of a loved voice caress'd –
A bolt is shot back somewhere in our breast,
And a lost pulse of feeling stirs again.
The eye sinks inward, and the heart lies plain,
And what we mean, we say, and what we would, we
    know.
A man becomes aware of his life's flow,
And hears its winding murmur; and he sees
The meadows where it glides, the sun, the breeze.

And there arrives a lull in the hot race
Wherein he doth for ever chase
That flying and elusive shadow, rest.
An air of coolness plays upon his face,
And an unwonted calm pervades his breast.
And then he thinks he knows
The hills where his life rose,
And the sea where it goes.

STANZAS FROM THE GRANDE CHARTREUSE

Through Alpine meadows soft-suffused
With rain, where thick the crocus blows,
Past the dark forges long disused,
The mule-track from Saint Laurent goes.
The bridge is cross'd, and slow we ride,
Through forest, up the mountain-side.

The autumnal evening darkens round,
The wind is up, and drives the rain;
While, hark! far down, with strangled sound
Doth the Dead Guier's stream complain,
Where that wet smoke, among the woods,
Over his boiling cauldron broods.

Swift rush the spectral vapours white
Past limestone scars with ragged pines,
Showing – then blotting from our sight! –
Halt – through the cloud-drift something shines!
High in the valley, wet and drear,
The huts of Courrerie appear.

Strike leftward! cries our guide; and higher
Mounts up the stony forest-way.
At last the encircling trees retire;
Look! through the showery twilight grey
What pointed roofs are these advance? –
A palace of the Kings of France?

Approach, for what we seek is here!
Alight, and sparely sup, and wait
For rest in this outbuilding near;
Then cross the sward and reach that gate.
Knock; pass the wicket! Thou art come
To the Carthusians' world-famed home.

The silent courts, where night and day
Into their stone-carved basins cold
The splashing icy fountains play –
The humid corridors behold!
Where, ghostlike in the deepening night,
Cowl'd forms brush by in gleaming white.

The chapel, where no organ's peal
Invests the stern and naked prayer –
With penitential cries they kneel
And wrestle; rising then, with bare
And white uplifted faces stand,
Passing the Host from hand to hand;

Each takes, and then his visage wan
Is buried in his cowl once more.
The cells! – the suffering Son of Man
Upon the wall – the knee-worn floor –
And where they sleep, that wooden bed,
Which shall their coffin be, when dead!

The library, where tract and tome
Not to feed priestly pride are there,
To hymn the conquering march of Rome,
Nor yet to amuse, as ours are!
They paint of souls the inner strife,
Their drops of blood, their death in life.

The garden, overgrown – yet mild,
See, fragrant herbs are flowering there!
Strong children of the Alpine wild
Whose culture is the brethren's care;
Of human tasks their only one,
And cheerful works beneath the sun.

Those halls, too, destined to contain
Each its own pilgrim-host of old,
From England, Germany, or Spain –
All are before me! I behold
The House, the Brotherhood austere!
 – And what am I, that I am here?

For rigorous teachers seized my youth,
And purged its faith, and trimm'd its fire,
Show'd me the high, white star of Truth,
There bade me gaze, and there aspire.
Even now their whispers pierce the gloom:
What dost thou in this living tomb?

Forgive me, masters of the mind!
At whose behest I long ago
So much unlearnt, so much resign'd –
I come not here to be your foe!
I seek these anchorites, not in ruth,
To curse and to deny your truth;

Not as their friend, or child, I speak!
But as, on some far northern strand,
Thinking of his own Gods, a Greek
In pity and mournful awe might stand
Before some fallen Runic stone –
For both were faiths, and both are gone.

Wandering between two worlds, one dead,
The other powerless to be born,
With nowhere yet to rest my head,
Like these, on earth I wait forlorn.
Their faith, my tears, the world deride –
I come to shed them at their side.

Oh, hide me in your gloom profound,
Ye solemn seats of holy pain!
Take me, cowl'd forms, and fence me round,
Till I possess my soul again;
Till free my thoughts before me roll,
Not chafed by hourly false control!

For the world cries your faith is now
But a dead time's exploded dream;
My melancholy, sciolists say,
Is a pass'd mode, an outworn theme –
As if the world had ever had
A faith, or sciolists been sad!

Ah, if it *be* pass'd, take away,
At least, the restlessness, the pain;
Be man henceforth no more a prey
To these out-dated stings again!
The nobleness of grief is gone –
Ah, leave us not the fret alone!

But – if you cannot give us ease –
Last of the race of them who grieve
Here leave us to die out with these
Last of the people who believe!
Silent, while years engrave the brow;
Silent – the best are silent now.

Achilles ponders in his tent,
The kings of modern thought are dumb;
Silent they are, though not content,
And wait to see the future come.
They have the grief men had of yore,
But they contend and cry no more.

Our fathers water'd with their tears
This sea of time whereon we sail,
Their voices were in all men's ears
Who pass'd within their puissant hail.
Still the same ocean round us raves,
But we stand mute, and watch the waves.

For what avail'd it, all the noise
And outcry of the former men? –
Say, have their sons achieved more joys,
Say, is life lighter now than then?
The sufferers died, they left their pain –
The pangs which tortured them remain.

What helps it now, that Byron bore,
With haughty scorn which mock'd the smart,
Through Europe to the Aetolian shore
The pageant of his bleeding heart?
That thousands counted every groan,
And Europe made his woe her own?

What boots it, Shelley! that the breeze
Carried thy lovely wail away,
Musical through Italian trees
Which fringe thy soft blue Spezzian bay?
Inheritors of thy distress
Have restless hearts one throb the less?

Or are we easier, to have read,
O Obermann! the sad, stern page,
Which tells us how thou hidd'st thy head
From the fierce tempest of thine age
In the lone brakes of Fontainebleau,
Or chalets near the Alpine snow?

Ye slumber in your silent grave! –
The world, which for an idle day
Grace to your mood of sadness gave,
Long since hath flung her weeds away.
The eternal trifler breaks your spell;
But we – we learnt your lore too well!

Years hence, perhaps, may dawn an age,
More fortunate, alas! than we,
Which without hardness will be sage,
And gay without frivolity.
Sons of the world, oh, speed those years;
But, while we wait, allow our tears!

Allow them! We admire with awe
The exulting thunder of your race;
You give the universe your law,
You triumph over time and space!
Your pride of life, your tireless powers,
We laud them, but they are not ours.

We are like children rear'd in shade
Beneath some old-world abbey wall,
Forgotten in a forest-glade,
And secret from the eyes of all.
Deep, deep the greenwood round them waves,
Their abbey, and its close of graves!

But, where the road runs near the stream,
Oft through the trees they catch a glance
Of passing troops in the sun's beam –
Pennon, and plume, and flashing lance!
Forth to the world those soldiers fare,
To life, to cities, and to war!

And through the wood, another way,
Faint bugle-notes from far are borne,
Where hunters gather, staghounds bay,
Round some fair forest-lodge at morn.
Gay dames are there, in sylvan green;
Laughter and cries – those notes between!

The banners flashing through the trees
Make their blood dance and chain their eyes
That bugle-music on the breeze
Arrests them with a charm'd surprise.
Banner by turns and bugle woo:
Ye shy recluses, follow too!

O children, what do ye reply? –
'Action and pleasure, will ye roam
Through these secluded dells to cry
And call us? – but too late ye come!
Too late for us your call ye blow,
Whose bent was taken long ago.

'Long since we pace this shadow'd nave;
We watch those yellow tapers shine,
Emblems of hope over the grave,
In the high altar's depth divine;
The organ carries to our ear
Its accents of another sphere.

'Fenced early in this cloistral round
Of reverie, of shade, of prayer,
How should we grow in other ground?
How can we flower in foreign air?
– Pass, banners, pass, and bugles, cease;
And leave our desert to its peace!'

From SOHRAB AND RUSTUM

. . .

So Rustum knew not his own loss, but stood
Over his dying son, and knew him not.
  But, with a cold incredulous voice, he said:–
'What prate is this of fathers and revenge?
The mighty Rustum never had a son.'
  And, with a failing voice, Sohrab replied:–
'Ah yes, he had! and that lost son am I.
Surely the news will one day reach his ear,
Reach Rustum, where he sits, and tarries long,
Somewhere, I know not where, but far from here;
And pierce him like a stab, and make him leap
To arms, and cry for vengeance upon thee.
Fierce man, bethink thee, for an only son!
What will that grief, what will that vengeance be?
Oh, could I live, till I that grief had seen!
Yet him I pity not so much, but her,
My mother, who in Ader-baijan dwells
With that old king, her father, who grows grey
With age, and rules over the valiant Koords.
Her most I pity, who no more will see
Sohrab returning from the Tartar camp,
With spoils and honour, when the war is done.
But a dark rumour will be bruited up,
From tribe to tribe, until it reach her ear;

And then will that defenceless woman learn
That Sohrab will rejoice her sight no more,
But that in battle with a nameless foe,
By the far-distant Oxus, he is slain.'

He spoke; and as he ceased, he wept aloud,
Thinking of her he left, and his own death.
He spoke; but Rustum listen'd, plunged in thought.
Nor did he yet believe it was his son
Who spoke, although he call'd back names he knew;
For he had had sure tidings that the babe,
Which was in Ader-baijan born to him,
Had been a puny girl, no boy at all –
So that sad mother sent him word, for fear
Rustum should seek the boy, to train in arms.
And so he deem'd that either Sohrab took,
By a false boast, the style of Rustum's son;
Or that men gave it him, to swell his fame.
So deem'd he; yet he listen'd, plunged in thought
And his soul set to grief, as the vast tide
Of the bright rocking Ocean sets to shore
At the full moon; tears gather'd in his eyes;
For he remember'd his own early youth,
And all its bounding rapture; as, at dawn,
The shepherd from his mountain-lodge descries
A far, bright city, smitten by the sun,
Through many rolling clouds – so Rustum saw

His youth; saw Sohrab's mother, in her bloom;
And that old king, her father, who loved well
His wandering guest, and gave him his fair child
With joy; and all the pleasant life they led,
They three, in that long-distant summer-time –
The castle, and the dewy woods, and hunt
And hound, and morn on those delightful hills
In Ader-baijan. And he saw that youth,
Of age and looks to be his own dear son,
Piteous and lovely, lying on the sand,
Like some rich hyacinth which by the scythe
Of an unskilful gardener has been cut,
Mowing the garden grass-plots near its bed,
And lies, a fragrant tower of purple bloom,
On the mown, dying grass – so Sohrab lay,
Lovely in death, upon the common sand.
And Rustum gazed on him with grief, and said:–

  'O Sohrab, thou indeed art such a son
Whom Rustum, wert thou his, might well have loved.
Yet here thou errest, Sohrab, or else men
Have told thee false – thou art not Rustum's son.
For Rustum had no son; one child he had –
But one – a girl; who with her mother now
Plies some light female task, nor dreams of us –
Of us she dreams not, nor of wounds, nor war.'

  But Sohrab answer'd him in wrath; for now

The anguish of the deep-fix'd spear grew fierce,
And he desired to draw forth the steel,
And let the blood flow free, and so to die –
But first he would convince his stubborn foe;
And, rising sternly on one arm, he said:–

'Man, who art thou who dost deny my words?
Truth sits upon the lips of dying men,
And falsehood, while I lived, was far from mine.
I tell thee, prick'd upon this arm I bear
That seal which Rustum to my mother gave,
That she might prick it on the babe she bore.'

He spoke; and all the blood left Rustum's cheeks,
And his knees totter'd, and he smote his hand
Against his breast, his heavy mailed hand,
That the hard iron corslet clank'd aloud;
And to his heart he press'd the other hand,
And in a hollow voice he spake, and said:–

'Sohrab, that were a proof which could not lie!
If thou show this, then art thou Rustum's son.'

Then, with weak hasty fingers, Sohrab loosed
His belt, and near the shoulder bared his arm,
And show'd a sign in faint vermilion points
Prick'd; as a cunning workman, in Pekin,
Pricks with vermilion some clear porcelain vase,
An emperor's gift – at early morn he paints,
And all day long, and, when night comes, the lamp

Lights up his studious forehead and thin hands –
So delicately prick'd the sign appear'd
On Sohrab's arm, the sign of Rustum's seal.
It was that griffin, which of old rear'd Zal,
Rustum's great father, whom they left to die,
A helpless babe, among the mountain-rocks;
Him that kind creature found, and rear'd, and loved –
Then Rustum took it for his glorious sign.
And Sohrab bared that image on his arm,
And himself scann'd it long with mournful eyes,
And then he touch'd it with his hand and said:–

   'How say'st thou? Is that sign the proper sign
Of Rustum's son, or of some other man's?'

   He spoke; but Rustum gazed, and gazed, and stood
Speechless; and then he utter'd one sharp cry:
O boy – *thy father!* – and his voice choked there.
And then a dark cloud pass'd before his eyes,
And his head swam, and he sank down to earth.
But Sohrab crawl'd to where he lay, and cast
His arms about his neck, and kiss'd his lips,
And with fond faltering fingers stroked his cheeks,
Trying to call him back to life; and life
Came back to Rustum, and he oped his eyes,
And they stood wide with horror; and he seized
In both his hands the dust which lay around,
And threw it on his head, and smirch'd his hair, –

His hair, and face, and beard, and glittering arms;
And strong convulsive groanings shook his breast,
And his sobs choked him; and he clutch'd his sword,
To draw it, and for ever let life out.
But Sohrab saw his thought, and held his hands,
And with a soothing voice he spake, and said:–
    'Father, forbear! for I but meet to-day
The doom which at my birth was written down
In Heaven, and thou art Heaven's unconscious hand.
Surely my heart cried out that it was thou,
When first I saw thee; and thy heart spoke too,
I know it! but fate trod those promptings down
Under its iron heel; fate, fate engaged
The strife, and hurl'd me on my father's spear.
But let us speak no more of this! I find
My father; let me feel that I have found!
Come, sit beside me on this sand, and take
My head betwixt thy hands, and kiss my cheeks,
And wash them with thy tears, and say: My son!
Quick! quick! for number'd are my sands of life,
And swift; for like the lightning to this field
I came, and like the wind I go away –
Sudden, and swift, and like a passing wind.
But it was writ in Heaven that this should be.'
    So said he, and his voice released the heart
Of Rustum, and his tears broke forth; he cast

His arms round his son's neck, and wept aloud,
And kiss'd him. And awe fell on both the hosts,
When they saw Rustum's grief; and Ruksh, the horse,
With his head bowing to the ground and mane
Sweeping the dust, came near, and in mute woe
First to the one then to the other moved
His head, as if inquiring what their grief
Might mean; and from his dark, compassionate eyes,
The big warm tears roll'd down, and caked the sand.
But Rustum chid him with stern voice, and said: –

'Ruksh, now thou grievest; but, O Ruksh, thy feet
Should first have rotted on their nimble joints,
Or ere they brought thy master to this field!'

But Sohrab look'd upon the horse and said:–
'Is this, then, Ruksh? How often, in past days,
My mother told me of thee, thou brave steed,
My terrible father's terrible horse! and said,
That I should one day find thy lord and thee.
Come, let me lay my hand upon thy mane!
O Ruksh, thou art more fortunate than I;
For thou hast gone where I shall never go,
And snuff'd the breezes of my father's home.
And thou hast trod the sands of Seistan,
And seen the River of Helmund, and the Lake
Of Zirrah; and the aged Zal himself
Has often stroked thy neck, and given thee food,

Corn in a golden platter soak'd with wine,
And said: *O Ruksh! bear Rustum well!* – but I
Have never known my grandsire's furrow'd face,
Nor seen his lofty house in Seistan,
Nor slaked my thirst at the clear Helmund stream;
But lodged among my father's foes, and seen
Afrasiab's cities only, Samarcand,
Bokhara, and lone Khiva in the waste,
And the black Toorkmun tents; and only drunk
The desert rivers, Moorghab and Tejend,
Kohik, and where the Kalmuks feed their sheep,
The northern Sir; and this great Oxus stream,
The yellow Oxus, by whose brink I die.'

Then, with a heavy groan, Rustum bewail'd: –
'Oh, that its waves were flowing over me!
Oh, that I saw its grains of yellow silt
Roll tumbling in the current o'er my head!'

But, with a grave mild voice, Sohrab replied: –
'Desire not that, my father! thou must live.
For some are born to do great deeds, and live,
As some are born to be obscured, and die.
Do thou the deeds I die too young to do,
And reap a second glory in thine age;
Thou art my father, and thy gain is mine.
But come! thou seest this great host of men
Which follow me; I pray thee, slay not these!
Let me entreat for them; what have they done?

They follow'd me, my hope, my fame, my star.
Let them all cross the Oxus back in peace.
But me thou must bear hence, not send with them,
But carry me with thee to Seistan,
And place me on a bed, and mourn for me,
Thou, and the snow-hair'd Zal, and all thy friends.
And thou must lay me in that lovely earth,
And heap a stately mound above my bones,
And plant a far-seen pillar over all.
That so the passing horseman on the waste
May see my tomb a great way off, and cry:
Sohrab, the mighty Rustum's son, lies there,
Whom his great father did in ignorance kill!
And I be not forgotten in my grave.'

　　And, with a mournful voice, Rustum replied: –
'Fear not! as thou hast said, Sohrab, my son,
So shall it be; for I will burn my tents,
And quit the host, and bear thee hence with me,
And carry thee away to Seistan,
And place thee on a bed, and mourn for thee,
With the snow-headed Zal, and all my friends.
And I will lay thee in that lovely earth,
And heap a stately mound above thy bones,
And plant a far-seen pillar over all,
And men shall not forget thee in thy grave.
And I will spare thy host; yea, let them go!
Let them all cross the Oxus back in peace!

What should I do with slaying any more?
For would that all whom I have ever slain
Might be once more alive; my bitterest foes,
And they who were call'd champions in their time,
And through whose death I won that fame I have –
And I were nothing but a common man,
A poor, mean soldier, and without renown,
So thou mightest live too, my son, my son!
Or rather would that I, even I myself,
Might now be lying on this bloody sand,
Near death, and by an ignorant stroke of thine,
Not thou of mine! and I might die, not thou;
And I, not thou, be borne to Seistan;
And Zal might weep above my grave, not thine;
And say: O son, I weep thee not too sore,
For willingly, I know, thou met'st thine end!
But now in blood and battles was my youth,
And full of blood and battles is my age,
And I shall never end this life of blood.'

    Then, at the point of death, Sohrab replied:–
'A life of blood indeed, thou dreadful man!
But thou shalt yet have peace; only not now,
Not yet! but thou shalt have it on that day,
When thou shalt sail in a high-masted ship,
Thou and the other peers of Kai Khosroo,
Returning home over the salt blue sea,

From laying thy dear master in his grave.'
    And Rustum gazed in Sohrab's face, and said:–
'Soon be that day, my son, and deep that sea!
Till then, if fate so wills, let me endure.'

    He spoke; and Sohrab smiled on him, and took
The spear, and drew it from his side, and eased
His wound's imperious anguish; but the blood
Came welling from the open gash, and life
Flow'd with the stream; – all down his cold white side
The crimson torrent ran, dim now and soil'd,
Like the soil'd tissue of white violets
Left, freshly gather'd, on their native bank,
By children whom their nurses call with haste
Indoors from the sun's eye; his head droop'd low,
His limbs grew slack; motionless, white, he lay –
White, with eyes closed; only when heavy gasps,
Deep heavy gasps quivering through all his frame,
Convulsed him back to life, he open'd them,
And fix'd them feebly on his father's face;
Till now all strength was ebb'd, and from his limbs
Unwillingly the spirit fled away,
Regretting the warm mansion which it left,
And youth, and bloom, and this delightful world.

    So, on the bloody sand, Sohrab lay dead;
And the great Rustum drew his horseman's cloak
Down o'er his face, and sate by his dead son.

As those black granite pillars, once high-rear'd
By Jemshid in Persepolis, to bear
His house, now 'mid their broken flights of steps
Lie prone, enormous, down the mountain side—
So in the sand lay Rustum by his son.

And night came down over the solemn waste,
And the two gazing hosts, and that sole pair,
And darken'd all; and a cold fog, with night,
Crept from the Oxus. Soon a hum arose,
As of a great assembly loosed, and fires
Began to twinkle through the fog; for now
Both armies moved to camp, and took their meal;
The Persians took it on the open sands
Southward, the Tartars by the river marge;
And Rustum and his son were left alone.

But the majestic river floated on,
Out of the mist and hum of that low land,
Into the frosty starlight, and there moved,
Rejoicing, through the hush'd Chorasmian waste,
Under the solitary moon; – he flow'd
Right for the polar star, past Orgunjè,
Brimming, and bright, and large; then sands begin
To hem his watery march, and dam his streams,
And split his currents; that for many a league
The shorn and parcell'd Oxus strains along
Through beds of sand and matted rushy isles—

Oxus, forgetting the bright speed he had
In his high mountain cradle in Pamere,
A foil'd circuitous wanderer – till at last
The long'd-for dash of waves is heard, and wide
His luminous home of waters opens, bright
And tranquil, from whose floor the new-bathed stars
Emerge, and shine upon the Aral Sea.

THE SCHOLAR-GIPSY

Go, for they call you, shepherd, from the hill;
　Go, shepherd, and untie the wattled cotes!
　　No longer leave thy wistful flock unfed,
　Nor let thy bawling fellows rack their throats,
　　Nor the cropp'd herbage shoot another head.
　　　But when the fields are still,
　And the tired men and dogs all gone to rest,
　　And only the white sheep are sometimes seen
　　Cross and recross the strips of moon-blanch'd
　　　　green,
Come, shepherd, and again begin the quest!

Here, where the reaper was at work of late –
　In this high field's dark corner, where he leaves
　　His coat, his basket, and his earthen cruse,
　And in the sun all morning binds the sheaves,
　　Then here, at noon, comes back his stores to use –
　　　Here will I sit and wait,
　While to my ear from uplands far away
　　The bleating of the folded flocks is borne,
　　With distant cries of reapers in the corn –
All the live murmur of a summer's day.

Screen'd is this nook o'er the high, half-reap'd field,
     And here till sun-down, shepherd! will I be.
          Through the thick corn the scarlet poppies peep,
     And round green roots and yellowing stalks I see
          Pale pink convolvulus in tendrils creep;
               And air-swept lindens yield
     Their scent, and rustle down their perfumed showers
          Of bloom on the bent grass where I am laid,
          And bower me from the August sun with shade;
     And the eye travels down to Oxford's towers.

And near me on the grass lies Glanvil's book—
     Come, let me read the oft-read tale again!
          The story of the Oxford scholar poor,
     Of pregnant parts and quick inventive brain,
          Who, tired of knocking at preferment's door,
               One summer-morn forsook
     His friends, and went to learn the gipsy-lore,
          And roam'd the world with that wild
               brotherhood,
          And came, as most men deem'd, to little good,
     But came to Oxford and his friends no more.

But once, years after, in the country-lanes,
  Two scholars, whom at college erst he knew,
    Met him, and of his way of life enquired;
Whereat he answer'd, that the gipsy-crew,
    His mates, had arts to rule as they desired
      The workings of men's brains,
And they can bind them to what thoughts they
    will.
  'And I,' he said, 'the secret of their art,
    When fully learn'd, will to the world impart;
But it needs heaven-sent moments for this skill.'

This said, he left them, and return'd no more. –
  But rumours hung about the country-side,
    That the lost Scholar long was seen to stray,
Seen by rare glimpses, pensive and tongue-tied,
    In hat of antique shape, and cloak of grey,
      The same the gipsies wore.
Shepherds had met him on the Hurst in spring;
    At some lone alehouse in the Berkshire moors,
    On the warm ingle-bench, the smock-frock'd
      boors
Had found him seated at their entering,

But, 'mid their drink and clatter, he would fly.
  And I myself seem half to know thy looks,
    And put the shepherds, wanderer! on thy trace;
  And boys who in lone wheatfields scare the rooks
    I ask if thou hast pass'd their quiet place;
      Or in my boat I lie
  Moor'd to the cool bank in the summer-heats,
    'Mid wide grass meadows which the sunshine fills,
    And watch the warm, green-muffled Cumner
      hills,
  And wonder if thou haunt'st their shy retreats.

For most, I know, thou lov'st retired ground!
  Thee at the ferry Oxford riders blithe,
    Returning home on summer-nights, have met
  Crossing the stripling Thames at Bab-lock-hithe,
    Trailing in the cool stream thy fingers wet,
      As the punt's rope chops round;
  And leaning backward in a pensive dream,
    And fostering in thy lap a heap of flowers
    Pluck'd in shy fields and distant Wychwood
      bowers,
  And thine eyes resting on the moonlit stream.

And then they land, and thou art seen no more! –
  Maidens, who from the distant hamlets come
    To dance around the Fyfield elm in May,
  Oft through the darkening fields have seen thee
        roam,
    Or cross a stile into the public way.
      Oft thou hast given them store
  Of flowers – the frail-leaf'd, white anemony,
    Dark bluebells drench'd with dews of summer
        eves,
    And purple orchises with spotted leaves –
  But none hath words she can report of thee.

And, above Godstow Bridge, when hay-time's here
  In June, and many a scythe in sunshine flames,
    Men who through those wide fields of breezy grass
  Where black-wing'd swallows haunt the glittering
        Thames,
    To bathe in the abandon'd lasher pass,
      Have often pass'd thee near
  Sitting upon the river bank o'ergrown;
    Mark'd thine outlandish garb, thy figure spare,
    Thy dark vague eyes, and soft abstracted air –
  But, when they came from bathing, thou wast gone!

At some lone homestead in the Cumner hills,
　　Where at her open door the housewife darns,
　　　Thou hast been seen, or hanging on a gate
　　To watch the threshers in the mossy barns.
　　　Children, who early range these slopes and late
　　　　For cresses from the rills,
　　Have known thee eying, all an April-day,
　　　The springing pastures and the feeding kine;
　　　And mark'd thee, when the stars come out and
　　　　shine,
Through the long dewy grass move slow away.

In autumn, on the skirts of Bagley Wood –
　　Where most the gipsies by the turf-edged way
　　　Pitch their smoked tents, and every bush you see
　　With scarlet patches tagg'd and shreds of grey,
　　　Above the forest-ground called Thessaly –
　　　　The blackbird, picking food,
　　Sees thee, nor stops his meal, nor fears at all;
　　　So often has he known thee past him stray,
　　　Rapt, twirling in thy hand a wither'd spray,
And waiting for the spark from heaven to fall.

And once, in winter, on the causeway chill
   Where home through flooded fields foot-travellers go,
      Have I not pass'd thee on the wooden bridge,
   Wrapt in thy cloak and battling with the snow,
      Thy face tow'rd Hinksey and its wintry ridge?
         And thou hast climb'd the hill,
   And gain'd the white brow of the Cumner range;
      Turn'd once to watch, while thick the snowflakes
         fall,
      The line of festal light in Christ-Church hall –
   Then sought thy straw in some sequester'd grange.

But what – I dream! Two hundred years are flown
   Since first thy story ran through Oxford halls,
      And the grave Glanvil did the tale inscribe
   That thou wert wander'd from the studious walls
      To learn strange arts, and join a gipsy-tribe;
         And thou from earth art gone
   Long since, and in some quiet churchyard laid –
      Some country-nook, where o'er thy unknown grave
      Tall grasses and white flowering nettles wave,
   Under a dark, red-fruited yew-tree's shade.

– No, no, thou hast not felt the lapse of hours!
  For what wears out the life of mortal men?
  'Tis that from change to change their being rolls;
'Tis that repeated shocks, again, again,
  Exhaust the energy of strongest souls
    And numb the elastic powers.
Till having used our nerves with bliss and teen,
  And tired upon a thousand schemes our wit,
  To the just-pausing Genius we remit
Our worn-out life, and are – what we have been.

Thou hast not lived, why should'st thou perish, so?
  Thou hadst *one* aim, *one* business, *one* desire;
    Else wert thou long since number'd with the
        dead!
  Else hadst thou spent, like other men, thy fire!
    The generations of thy peers are fled,
      And we ourselves shall go;
But thou possessest an immortal lot,
  And we imagine thee exempt from age
  And living as thou liv'st on Glanvil's page,
Because thou hadst – what we, alas! have not.

For early didst thou leave the world, with powers
  Fresh, undiverted to the world without,
    Firm to their mark, not spent on other things;
  Free from the sick fatigue, the languid doubt,
    Which much to have tried, in much been baffled,
      brings.
      O life unlike to ours!
  Who fluctuate idly without term or scope,
    Of whom each strives, nor knows for what he
      strives,
    And each half lives a hundred different lives;
  Who wait like thee, but not, like thee, in hope.

Thou waitest for the spark from heaven! and we,
  Light half-believers of our casual creeds,
    Who never deeply felt, nor clearly will'd,
  Whose insight never has borne fruit in deeds,
    Whose vague resolves never have been fulfill'd;
      For whom each year we see
  Breeds new beginnings, disappointments new;
    Who hesitate and falter life away,
    And lose to-morrow the ground won to-day –
  Ah! do not we, wanderer! await it too?

Yes, we await it! – but it still delays,
  And then we suffer! and amongst us one,
    Who most has suffer'd, takes dejectedly
  His seat upon the intellectual throne;
    And all his store of sad experience he
      Lays bare of wretched days;
  Tells us his misery's birth and growth and signs,
    And how the dying spark of hope was fed,
    And how the breast was soothed, and how the
        head,
  And all his hourly varied anodynes.

This for our wisest! and we others pine,
  And wish the long unhappy dream would end,
    And waive all claim to bliss, and try to bear;
  With close-lipp'd patience for our only friend,
    Sad patience, too near neighbour to despair –
      But none has hope like thine!
  Thou through the fields and through the woods
        dost stray,
    Roaming the country-side, a truant boy,
    Nursing thy project in unclouded joy,
  And every doubt long blown by time away.

O born in days when wits were fresh and clear,
   And life ran gaily as the sparkling Thames;
     Before this strange disease of modern life,
   With its sick hurry, its divided aims,
      Its heads o'ertax'd, its palsied hearts, was rife –
       Fly hence, our contact, fear!
   Still fly, plunge deeper in the bowering wood!
     Averse, as Dido did with gesture stern
     From her false friend's approach in Hades turn,
Wave us away, and keep thy solitude!

Still nursing the unconquerable hope,
   Still clutching the inviolable shade,
     With a free, onward impulse brushing through,
   By night, the silver'd branches of the glade –
      Far on the forest-skirts, where none pursue,
       On some mild pastoral slope
Emerge, and resting on the moonlit pales
   Freshen thy flowers as in former years
     With dew, or listen with enchanted ears,
From the dark dingles, to the nightingales!

But fly our paths, our feverish contact fly!
  For strong the infection of our mental strife,
    Which, though it gives no bliss, yet spoils for rest;
  And we should win thee from thy own fair life,
    Like us distracted, and like us unblest.
      Soon, soon thy cheer would die,
  Thy hopes grow timorous, and unfix'd thy powers,
    And thy clear aims be cross and shifting made;
    And then thy glad perennial youth would fade,
Fade, and grow old at last, and die like ours.

Then fly our greetings, fly our speech and smiles!
  – As some grave Tyrian trader, from the sea,
    Descried at sunrise an emerging prow
  Lifting the cool-hair'd creepers stealthily,
    The fringes of a southward-facing brow
      Among the Aegaean isles;
  And saw the merry Grecian coaster come,
    Freighted with amber grapes, and Chian wine,
    Green, bursting figs and tunnies steep'd in brine –
And knew the intruders on his ancient home,

The young light-hearted masters of the waves –
    And snatch'd his rudder, and shook out more sail;
    And day and night held on indignantly
O'er the blue Midland waters with the gale,
    Betwixt the Syrtes and soft Sicily,
        To where the Atlantic raves
Outside the western straits; and unbent sails
    There, where down cloudy cliffs, through sheets
        of foam,
    Shy traffickers, the dark Iberians come;
And on the beach undid his corded bales.

RUGBY CHAPEL
November 1857

Coldly, sadly descends
The autumn-evening. The field
Strewn with its dank yellow drifts
Of wither'd leaves, and the elms,
Fade into dimness apace,
Silent; – hardly a shout
From a few boys late at their play!
The lights come out in the street,
In the school-room windows; – but cold,
Solemn, unlighted, austere,
Through the gathering darkness, arise
The chapel-walls, in whose bound
Thou, my father! art laid.

There thou dost lie, in the gloom
Of the autumn evening. But ah!
That word, *gloom*, to my mind
Brings thee back, in the light
Of thy radiant vigour, again;

In the gloom of November we pass'd
Days not dark at thy side;
Seasons impair'd not the ray
Of thy buoyant cheerfulness clear.
Such thou wast! and I stand
In the autumn evening, and think
Of bygone autumns with thee.

Fifteen years have gone round
Since thou arosest to tread,
In the summer-morning, the road
Of death, at a call unforeseen,
Sudden. For fifteen years,
We who till then in thy shade
Rested as under the boughs
Of a mighty oak, have endured
Sunshine and rain as we might,
Bare, unshaded, alone,
Lacking the shelter of thee.

O strong soul, by what shore
Tarriest thou now? For that force,
Surely, has not been left vain!
Somewhere, surely, afar,
In the sounding labour-house vast
Of being, is practised that strength,
Zealous, beneficent, firm!

Yes, in some far-shining sphere,
Conscious or not of the past,
Still thou performest the word
Of the Spirit in whom thou dost live –
Prompt, unwearied, as here!
Still thou upraisest with zeal
The humble good from the ground,
Sternly repressest the bad!
Still, like a trumpet, dost rouse
Those who with half-open eyes
Tread the border-land dim
'Twixt vice and virtue; reviv'st,
Succourest! – this was thy work,
This was thy life upon earth.

What is the course of the life
Of mortal men on the earth? –
Most men eddy about
Here and there – eat and drink,
Chatter and love and hate,
Gather and squander, are raised
Aloft, are hurl'd in the dust,
Striving blindly, achieving
Nothing; and then they die –
Perish; – and no one asks
Who or what they have been,

More than he asks what waves,
In the moonlit solitudes mild
Of the midmost Ocean, have swell'd,
Foam'd for a moment, and gone.

And there are some, whom a thirst
Ardent, unquenchable, fires,
Not with the crowd to be spent,
Not without aim to go round
In an eddy of purposeless dust,
Effort unmeaning and vain.
Ah yes! some of us strive
Not without action to die
Fruitless, but something to snatch
From dull oblivion, nor all
Glut the devouring grave!
We, we have chosen our path –
Path to a clear-purposed goal,
Path of advance! – but it leads
A long, steep journey, through sunk
Gorges, o'er mountains in snow.
Cheerful, with friends, we set forth –
Then, on the height, comes the storm.

Thunder crashes from rock
To rock, the cataracts reply,
Lightnings dazzle our eyes.
Roaring torrents have breach'd
The track, the stream-bed descends
In the place where the wayfarer once
Planted his footstep – the spray
Boils o'er its borders! aloft
The unseen snow-beds dislodge
Their hanging ruin; alas,
Havoc is made in our train!
Friends, who set forth at our side,
Falter, are lost in the storm.
We, we only are left!
With frowning foreheads, with lips
Sternly compress'd, we strain on,
On – and at nightfall at last
Come to the end of our way,
To the lonely inn 'mid the rocks;
Where the gaunt and taciturn host
Stands on the threshold, the wind
Shaking his thin white hairs –
Holds his lantern to scan
Our storm-beat figures, and asks:
Whom in our party we bring?
Whom we have left in the snow?

Sadly we answer: We bring
Only ourselves! we lost
Sight of the rest in the storm.
Hardly ourselves we fought through,
Stripp'd, without friends, as we are.
Friends, companions, and train,
The avalanche swept from our side.

But thou would'st not *alone*
Be saved, my father! *alone*
Conquer and come to thy goal,
Leaving the rest in the wild.

We were weary, and we
Fearful, and we in our march
Fain to drop down and to die.
Still thou turnedst, and still
Beckonedst the trembler, and still
Gavest the weary thy hand.

If, in the paths of the world,
Stones might have wounded thy feet,
Toil or dejection have tried
Thy spirit, of that we saw
Nothing – to us thou wast still
Cheerful, and helpful, and firm!
Therefore to thee it was given
Many to save with thyself;

And, at the end of thy day,
O faithful shepherd! to come,
Bringing thy sheep in thy hand.

And through thee I believe
In the noble and great who are gone;
Pure souls honour'd and blest
By former ages, who else –
Such, so soulless, so poor,
Is the race of men whom I see –
Seem'd but a dream of the heart,
Seem'd but a cry of desire.
Yes! I believe that there lived
Others like thee in the past,
Not like the men of the crowd
Who all round me to-day
Bluster or cringe, and make life
Hideous, and arid, and vile;
But souls temper'd with fire,
Fervent, heroic, and good,
Helpers and friends of mankind.

Servants of God! – or sons
Shall I not call you? because
Not as servants ye knew
Your Father's innermost mind,

His, who unwillingly sees
One of his little ones lost –
Yours is the praise, if mankind
Hath not as yet in its march
Fainted, and fallen, and died!

See! In the rocks of the world
Marches the host of mankind,
A feeble, wavering line.
Where are they tending? – A God
Marshall'd them, gave them their goal.
Ah, but the way is so long!
Years they have been in the wild!
Sore thirst plagues them, the rocks,
Rising all round, overawe;
Factions divide them, their host
Threatens to break, to dissolve.
– Ah, keep, keep them combined!
Else, of the myriads who fill
That army, not one shall arrive;
Sole they shall stray; in the rocks
Stagger for ever in vain,
Die one by one in the waste.

Then, in such hour of need
Of your fainting, dispirited race,

Ye, like angels, appear,
Radiant with ardour divine!
Beacons of hope, ye appear!
Languor is not in your heart,
Weakness is not in your word,
Weariness not on your brow.
Ye alight in our van! at your voice,
Panic, despair, flee away.
Ye move through the ranks, recall
The stragglers, refresh the outworn,
Praise, re-inspire the brave!
Order, courage, return.
Eyes rekindling, and prayers,
Follow your steps as ye go.
Ye fill up the gaps in our files,
Strengthen the wavering line,
Stablish, continue our march,
On, to the bound of the waste,
On, to the City of God.

THYRSIS

A MONODY, *to commemorate the author's friend,*
ARTHUR HUGH CLOUGH, *who died at Florence*, 1861

How changed is here each spot man makes or fills!
  In the two Hinkseys nothing keeps the same;
    The village street its haunted mansion lacks,
    And from the sign is gone Sibylla's name,
      And from the roofs the twisted chimney-stacks –
      Are ye too changed, ye hills?
    See, 'tis no foot of unfamiliar men
      To-night from Oxford up your pathway strays!
      Here came I often, often, in old days –
  Thyrsis and I; we still had Thyrsis then.

Runs it not here, the track by Childsworth Farm,
  Past the high wood, to where the elm-tree crowns
    The hill behind whose ridge the sunset flames?
  The signal-elm, that looks on Ilsley Downs,
      The Vale, the three lone weirs, the youthful
        Thames? –
      This winter-eve is warm,
    Humid the air! leafless, yet soft as spring,
      The tender purple spray on copse and briers!
      And that sweet city with her dreaming spires,
  She needs not June for beauty's heightening,

114

Lovely all times she lies, lovely to-night! –
  Only, methinks, some loss of habit's power
    Befalls me wandering through this upland dim.
  Once pass'd I blindfold here, at any hour;
    Now seldom come I, since I came with him.
      That single elm-tree bright
  Against the west – I miss it! is it gone?
    We prized it dearly; while it stood, we said,
    Our friend, the Gipsy-Scholar, was not dead;
  While the tree lived, he in these fields lived on.

Too rare, too rare, grow now my visits here,
  But once I knew each field, each flower, each stick;
    And with the country-folk acquaintance made
  By barn in threshing-time, by new-built rick.
    Here, too, our shepherd-pipes we first assay'd.
      Ah me! this many a year
  My pipe is lost, my shepherd's holiday!
    Needs must I lose them, needs with heavy heart
    Into the world and wave of men depart;
  But Thyrsis of his own will went away.

It irk'd him to be here, he could not rest.
 He loved each simple joy the country yields,
  He loved his mates; but yet he could not keep,
 For that a shadow lour'd on the fields,
  Here with the shepherds and the silly sheep.
   Some life of men unblest
 He knew, which made him droop, and fill'd his head.
  He went; his piping took a troubled sound
  Of storms that rage outside our happy ground;
 He could not wait their passing, he is dead.

So, some tempestuous morn in early June,
 When the year's primal burst of bloom is o'er,
  Before the roses and the longest day –
 When garden-walks and all the grassy floor
  With blossoms red and white of fallen May
   And chestnut-flowers are strewn –
 So have I heard the cuckoo's parting cry,
  From the wet field, through the vext garden-trees,
  Come with the volleying rain and tossing breeze:
 The bloom is gone, and with the bloom go I!

Too quick despairer, wherefore wilt thou go?
   Soon will the high Midsummer pomps come on,
      Soon will the musk carnations break and swell,
Soon shall we have gold-dusted snapdragon,
      Sweet-William with his homely cottage-smell,
         And stocks in fragrant blow;
Roses that down the alleys shine afar,
      And open, jasmine-muffled lattices,
      And groups under the dreaming garden-trees,
And the full moon, and the white evening-star.

He hearkens not! light comer, he is flown!
   What matters it? next year he will return,
      And we shall have him in the sweet spring-days,
With whitening hedges, and uncrumpling fern,
      And blue-bells trembling by the forest-ways,
         And scent of hay new-mown.
But Thyrsis never more we swains shall see;
      See him come back, and cut a smoother reed,
      And blow a strain the world at last shall heed –
For Time, not Corydon, hath conquer'd thee!

Alack, for Corydon no rival now! –
    But when Sicilian shepherds lost a mate,
        Some good survivor with his flute would go,
    Piping a ditty sad for Bion's fate;
        And cross the unpermitted ferry's flow,
            And relax Pluto's brow,
    And make leap up with joy the beauteous head
        Of Proserpine, among whose crowned hair
        Are flowers first open'd on Sicilian air,
    And flute his friend, like Orpheus, from the dead.

O easy access to the hearer's grace
    When Dorian shepherds sang to Proserpine!
        For she herself had trod Sicilian fields,
    She knew the Dorian water's gush divine,
        She knew each lily white which Enna yields,
            Each rose with blushing face;
    She loved the Dorian pipe, the Dorian strain.
        But ah, of our poor Thames she never heard!
        Her foot the Cumner cowslips never stirr'd;
    And we should tease her with our plaint in vain!

Well! wind-dispersed and vain the words will be,
    Yet, Thyrsis, let me give my grief its hour
        In the old haunt, and find our tree-topp'd hill!
    Who, if not I, for questing here hath power?
        I know the wood which hides the daffodil,
            I know the Fyfield tree,
    I know what white, what purple fritillaries
        The grassy harvest of the river-fields,
        Above by Ensham, down by Sandford, yields,
    And what sedged brooks are Thames's tributaries;

I know these slopes; who knows them if not I? –
    But many a dingle on the loved hill-side,
        With thorns once studded, old, white-blossom'd
            trees,
    Where thick the cowslips grew, and far descried
        High tower'd the spikes of purple orchises,
            Hath since our day put by
    The coronals of that forgotten time;
        Down each green bank hath gone the ploughboy's
            team,
        And only in the hidden brookside gleam
    Primroses, orphans of the flowery prime.

Where is the girl, who by the boatman's door,
  Above the locks, above the boating throng,
    Unmoor'd our skiff when through the Wytham
        flats,
  Red loosestrife and blond meadow-sweet among
    And darting swallows and light water-gnats,
      We track'd the shy Thames shore?
Where are the mowers, who, as the tiny swell
  Of our boat passing heaved the river-grass,
  Stood with suspended scythe to see us pass? –
They all are gone, and thou art gone as well!

Yes, thou art gone! and round me too the night
  In ever-nearing circle weaves her shade.
    I see her veil draw soft across the day,
  I feel her slowly chilling breath invade
    The cheek grown thin, the brown hair sprent with
        grey;
      I feel her finger light
  Laid pausefully upon life's headlong train; –
    The foot less prompt to meet the morning dew,
    The heart less bounding at emotion new,
  And hope, once crush'd, less quick to spring again.

And long the way appears, which seem'd so short
    To the less practised eye of sanguine youth;
        And high the mountain-tops, in cloudy air,
    The mountain-tops where is the throne of Truth,
        Tops in life's morning-sun so bright and bare!
            Unbreachable the fort
    Of the long-batter'd world uplifts its wall;
        And strange and vain the earthly turmoil grows,
        And near and real the charm of thy repose,
    And night as welcome as a friend would fall.

But hush! the upland hath a sudden loss
    Of quiet! – Look, adown the dusk hill-side,
        A troop of Oxford hunters going home,
    As in old days, jovial and talking, ride!
        From hunting with the Berkshire hounds they
            come.
            Quick! let me fly, and cross
    Into yon farther field! – 'Tis done; and see,
        Back'd by the sunset, which doth glorify
        The orange and pale violet evening-sky,
    Bare on its lonely ridge, the Tree! the Tree!

I take the omen! Eve lets down her veil,
   The white fog creeps from bush to bush about,
      The west unflushes, the high stars grow bright,
   And in the scatter'd farms the lights come out.
      I cannot reach the signal-tree to-night,
         Yet, happy omen, hail!
   Hear it from thy broad lucent Arno-vale
      (For there thine earth-forgetting eyelids keep
      The morningless and unawakening sleep
   Under the flowery oleanders pale),

Hear it, O Thyrsis, still our tree is there! –
   Ah, vain! These English fields, this upland dim,
      These brambles pale with mist engarlanded,
      That lone, sky-pointing tree, are not for him;
   To a boon southern country he is fled,
         And now in happier air,
   Wandering with the great Mother's train divine
      (And purer or more subtle soul than thee,
      I trow, the mighty Mother doth not see)
   Within a folding of the Apennine,

Thou hearest the immortal chants of old! –
  Putting his sickle to the perilous grain
    In the hot cornfield of the Phrygian king,
  For thee the Lityerses-song again
    Young Daphnis with his silver voice doth sing;
      Sings his Sicilian fold,
  His sheep, his hapless love, his blinded eyes –
    And how a call celestial round him rang,
    And heavenward from the fountain-brink he
        sprang,
  And all the marvel of the golden skies.

There thou art gone, and me thou leavest here
  Sole in these fields! yet will I not despair.
    Despair I will not, while I yet descry
  'Neath the mild canopy of English air
    That lonely tree against the western sky.
      Still, still, these slopes, 'tis clear,
  Our Gipsy-Scholar haunts, outliving thee!
    Fields where soft sheep from cages pull the hay,
    Woods with anemonies in flower till May,
  Know him a wanderer still; then why not me?

A fugitive and gracious light he seeks,
  Shy to illumine; and I seek it too.
    This does not come with houses or with gold,
  With place, with honour, and a flattering crew;
    'Tis not in the world's market bought and sold –
      But the smooth-slipping weeks
  Drop by, and leave its seeker still untired;
    Out of the heed of mortals he is gone,
    He wends unfollow'd, he must house alone;
  Yet on he fares, by his own heart inspired.

Thou too, O Thyrsis, on like quest wast bound;
  Thou wanderedst with me for a little hour!
    Men gave thee nothing; but this happy quest,
  If men esteem'd thee feeble, gave thee power,
    If men procured thee trouble, gave thee rest.
      And this rude Cumner ground,
  Its fir-topped Hurst, its farms, its quiet fields,
    Here camst thou in thy jocund youthful time,
    Here was thine height of strength, thy golden
        prime!
  And still the haunt beloved a virtue yields.

What though the music of thy rustic flute
   Kept not for long its happy, country tone;
      Lost it too soon, and learnt a stormy note
Of men contention-tost, of men who groan,
      Which task'd thy pipe too sore, and tired thy
            throat –
         It fail'd, and thou wast mute!
Yet hadst thou alway visions of our light,
      And long with men of care thou couldst not stay,
      And soon thy foot resumed its wandering way,
Left human haunt, and on alone till night.

Too rare, too rare, grow now my visits here!
   'Mid city-noise, not, as with thee of yore,
      Thyrsis! in reach of sheep-bells is my home.
– Then through the great town's harsh, heart-
            wearying roar,
      Let in thy voice a whisper often come,
         To chase fatigue and fear:
      Why faintest thou? I wander'd till I died.
      Roam on! The light we sought is shining still.
      Dost thou ask proof? Our tree yet crowns the hill,
   Our Scholar travels yet the loved hill-side.

GROWING OLD

What is it to grow old?
Is it to lose the glory of the form,
The lustre of the eye?
Is it for beauty to forego her wreath?
– Yes, but not this alone.

Is it to feel our strength –
Not our bloom only, but our strength – decay?
Is it to feel each limb
Grow stiffer, every function less exact,
Each nerve more loosely strung?

Yes, this, and more; but not
Ah, 'tis not what in youth we dream'd 'twould be!
'Tis not to have our life
Mellow'd and soften'd as with sunset-glow,
A golden day's decline.

'Tis not to see the world
As from a height, with rapt prophetic eyes,
And heart profoundly stirr'd;
And weep, and feel the fulness of the past,
The years that are no more.

It is to spend long days
And not once feel that we were ever young;
It is to add, immured
In the hot prison of the present, month
To month with weary pain.

It is to suffer this,
And feel but half, and feebly, what we feel.
Deep in our hidden heart
Festers the dull remembrance of a change,
But no emotion – none.

It is – last stage of all –
When we are frozen up within, and quite
The phantom of ourselves,
To hear the world applaud the hollow ghost
Which blamed the living man.